SITTING IN:
ROCK PIANO
Backing Tracks and Improv Lessons

LOREN GOLD

D1613648

About the Audio Tracks and TNT² Software

Included with this book are companion MP3 play-along and demonstration tracks, and Alfred's exclusive TNT 2 software. TNT 2 allows users to customize audio tracks for practice. Use it to slow down tracks, isolate and loop parts, and change tempos and keys.

The audio and software content are available online to stream or download. Please see the enclosed insert card on the inside back cover for information on how to access the audio tracks and TNT 2 installer files.

TNT 2 SYSTEM REQUIREMENTS

Windows
7, 8, 10
QuickTime 7.6.7 or higher
1.8 GHz processor or faster
800 MB hard drive space
2 GB RAM minimum
Speakers or headphones
Internet access for updates

Macintosh
OS 10.4 and higher (Intel only)
QuickTime 7.6.7 or higher
900 MB hard drive space
2 GB RAM minimum
Speakers or headphones
Internet access for updates

Alfred Music
P.O. Box 10003
Van Nuys, CA 91410-0003
alfred.com

ISBN-10: 1-4706-1557-6 (Book & Online Audio/Software)
ISBN-13: 978-1-4706-1557-4 (Book & Online Audio/Software)

Basic audio tracks recorded at Alfred Road Studio, Van Nuys, CA. Loren Gold (piano), Brian Gallagher (saxophone), Brad Craig (guitar), Jon Button (bass), and Randy Cooke (drums). Brad Craig uses Scuffham S-Gear software guitar amps.

Cover Photos
Saxophonist: © Digital Vision • Keyboardist on Hammond B3: wikimedia / JacoTen and © Getty Images / mmac72
Keyboardist on piano: © Dale Berman • Keyboardist on Rhodes: wikimedia / MartinK • Guitarist: © iStockphoto / Jan Kowalski •
Bassist: © iStockphoto / Rapid Eye Media • Drummer: © iStockphoto / Aleksandar Georgiev
Author photo: © Carlos Lopez • Concert photo: © Hiroki Nishioka

Interior Photos
Billy Preston: wikimedia / Heinrich Klaffs • Jerry Lee Lewis: wikimedia / Silvio Tanaka •
Elton John: wikimedia / Heinrich Klaffs • Rick Wakeman: wikimedia / Aurelio Moraes

 Alfred Cares. Contents printed on environmentally responsible paper.

CONTENTS

ABOUT THE AUTHOR

Loren Gold is a Los Angeles-based keyboardist, vocalist, and songwriter who has worked extensively with pop, rock, and soul acts. Classically trained from age seven, Gold has also studied ragtime, blues, rock, gospel, and R&B. After many years writing, recording, and performing, he started touring with various artists in original bands. Gold began touring with Roger Daltrey in 2009, and in 2012, Gold joined The Who as keyboardist and vocalist.

Gold has also worked with Kenny Loggins, Natalie Maines (Dixie Chicks), and Don Felder (Eagles), among others, and served as musical director for Selena Gomez, Demi Lovato, and American Idol winner Taylor Hicks. In addition to touring and session work, Gold has composed original music for feature films and television, and has released instructional books with Alfred Music.

More information is available at:
lorengold.com

PHOTO © CARLOS LOPEZ

Acknowledgements

I would like to thank my family for their continued love and support. Thanks to the wonderful musicians who played on this recording: Randy Cooke, Jon Button, Brad Craig, and our dear friend Brian Gallagher, who passed away just a few days after our recording session. I feel so fortunate to have been blessed one final time with his beautiful saxophone. We miss you.

Special thanks to Mark Fried of Spirit Music Group. Thanks to the boys in The Who for continually inspiring me. Special thanks to Alfred Music for all their continued support and especially the close team that helped get this off the ground—Ron, Link, and Matt: you ROCK!

 In addition to TNT 2 software (with its own embedded audio tracks), MP3s are also included with this book. The symbol shown to the left appears next to every song in the book and is used to identify the TNT 2 tracks and MP3s that are accessible online.

For more information on TNT 2, visit:

alfred.com/TNT2

INTRODUCTION

Rock music covers such a wide range of styles and elements. Generally, when we hear "rock" we tend to think of heavy, loud music by bands like Led Zeppelin, The Who, and Deep Purple, but there are many different types of rock. If you go back to the early days of rock and roll, the piano (or sometimes the saxophone) was frequently the lead instrument—a setup rooted in blues music, which we covered in my first book, *Sitting In: Blues Piano*. As the years went on, the rock and roll sound became bigger, and yes, even louder at times. We transitioned from acoustic bass to electric bass, from one acoustic guitar to two electric guitars, from a piano to a synthesizer and organ, and from a washboard to a large, double-bass drum kit! Most of the time, music that is not jazz, classical, country, or hip-hop would typically fall into the "rock" or "rock and roll" category.

In this book, I've covered many of the great rock and roll keyboardists—from the 1950s sounds of Johnnie Johnson (Chuck Berry) to the playing of Ray Manzarek (The Doors), Jon Lord (Deep Purple), Billy Joel, and Elton John. Classic rock piano sounds of the 1970s and '80s are covered as well. *Sitting In: Rock Piano* provides tons of tips, riffs, and insights into how to approach improvising over rock music with a band. Enjoy, and rock on!

HOW TO USE THIS BOOK

Each section starts with a notated arrangement of the piece and is followed by a Roadmap, which tells you the exact layout of the tune from the audio recording.

Following the Roadmap is an Overview. This section addresses the key signature, beats per measure (bpm), number of bars, feel, scales, and types of voicings used in the piece.

Next comes Listening Suggestions, one of the most important parts of each section. When you look at an unknown piece, with no reference other than the feel and style notes, you can often miss subtleties that the composer might have had in mind. The Listening Suggestions sections can help tremendously—primarily for feel but also for what the composer may have used for inspiration. There is nothing wrong with sitting down and listening to the song suggestions first, just to get in a proper state of mind. This will also help inspire direction. If the Listening Suggestion says "Ray Manzarek," I'm going to listen to some Ray and then walk over to the piano. It can't hurt, right? Plus, this will broaden your eyes and ears. You'll find song references from some of the pioneers of rock and roll and modern artists as well. So, try sitting back and listening to some of these great artists before you dive in to the songs themselves.

After Listening Suggestions are the Fingering sections, which provide both right-hand and left-hand fingerings. Following that is Pocket, which addresses the chords, rhythmic feel, and accompaniment for the piece. This is followed by the Soloing section, featuring various licks that can be used to improvise over the song.

As a final thought, remember, the Listening Suggestions, audio examples, and licks should be used as guides. I encourage you to break any traditional rules, test the waters, and play from the heart. Also, if it sounds good to you, it probably is!

WORKING WITH THE AUDIO TRACKS AND SOFTWARE

Included with this book are three audio options for maximum versatility in your practicing. These tracks are available to download or stream for free with the purchase of the book. You get the following:

- An MP3 recording of each tune with a full band, including piano, guitar, saxophone, bass, and drums
- An MP3 recording of each tune with the band minus the piano
- TNT 2 software, which lets you isolate and loop sections, choose which instruments you want in the mix, and even change tempos and keys

In each case, you get multiple choruses of each song, played by a top-notch professional rock band. Each song contains a statement of the written arrangement (or "head"), followed by various solos, depending on the tune, before the head is restated. The length of each of these sections is laid out in the Roadmap that follows each song in the book.

The first set of MP3s (with keyboard solos) acts more as a demonstration and less as a play-along, with the piano offering some straightforward soloing and comping ideas and examples of what you can play over these tracks.

The second set of MP3s (without keyboard solos) contains the backing tracks. Here, you play the head. The guitar and saxophone solos provide some stylistically appropriate soloing ideas while giving you additional opportunity to comp for a soloist. Then, there is space for you to play the solo.

Alfred's TNT 2 software is the perfect practice tool. You can customize the song by choosing which instruments are in the mix. A transposition option allows you to try the songs out in different keys, while the tempo-changing feature can slow down the tempos of the songs or speed them up. For more information, visit alfred.com/TNT2.

Track 1 (Full Mix)
Track 1A (Rhythm Section Only)

WHISKEY LIGHTS

Roadmap

1 chorus of head, 2 choruses of keyboard solo, 2 choruses of guitar solo, 1 chorus of head, coda.

Overview

This tune is a throwback to the late 1960s, when Flower Power ruled the land. Ideally, this tune is to be played on an organ (something vintage like a Vox Continental or Farfisa would be great). "Whiskey Lights" is unique in the sense that you don't have to worry about interfering with the bass player, because you *are* the bass player in this song. This was the approach of The Doors keyboardist Ray Manzarek, who wrote and played bass lines on the organ!

- Key: E Minor
- BPM: 122
- Bars: 44
- Feel: 1960s organ rock
- Scale: E Dorian

Listening Suggestions

The Doors: "Light My Fire"
With one of the most famous organ intros ever, "Light My Fire" became The Doors' signature song and is a staple of the sound of the '60s. There are not many songs that capture the mood and imagery of a specific time period like this one does. I love how the right- and left-hand parts are so defined individually. When you put them together, you've got half your band right there. After you finish this book, go learn this song!

Right-Hand Fingering

Part 1

B, E, G: 1, 2, 4
C♯, E, A: 1, 2, 5

Part 2

G, C, E: 1, 2, 4
G, B, D: 1, 2, 3
A, D, F♯: 1, 2, 4
B, D, G: 1, 2, 5
F♯, B, D♯: 1, 2, 4

Left-Hand Fingering

Part 1

E, E, B, D, B, G: 1, 1, 2, 1, 2, 4
A, A, E, G, E, A: 1, 1, 2, 1, 2, 5

Part 2

Every four-note pattern (except
B Major chord*): 5, 3, 1
*B, D♯, F♯: 4, 3, 1

Riff over A Chord

Right Hand

E, G, E, D (use 2 on E♭ grace note): 3, 5, 3, 2

Left Hand

E, G, E, D: 2, 1, 2, 3

Pocket

Get in your time machine, and head back to the 1960s peace and love. Think The Doors, Ray Manzarek, and the Vox Continental organ. The right-hand part in "Whiskey Lights" emphasizes accents and pushes, while the left hand is the bass line, literally. The initial theme produces two distinct parts, while the B section is more uniform, played primarily on the downbeat.

Chords in the Tune

Em, A, A7, C, G, D, G/D, B

Soloing

The left-hand bass part is constant throughout this tune, which leaves the right hand free to explore mixing and matching various rhythms, ideas, and patterns to create something unique each time around. Lick 4 features some rhythms not used in the recording, but they could be used in a solo for this song. The key is to blend all of these ideas together when soloing.

Lick 1

This lick is an example of how you might start a solo, but it's nothing wild or too far removed from the feel of the song. I've broken out a bit from the Dorian mode by adding a bluesy, flat-5 note (B♭) for a very brief moment. We return to the original mode, with B-natural, in the next bar.

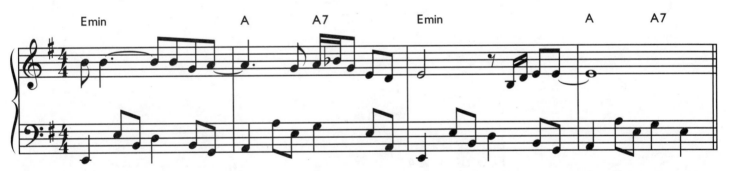

Lick 2

This has a similar feel to Lick 1, but it's a little trickier. Keep the left-hand pattern solid, and play around with the right hand by accenting different parts of the beat.

Lick 3

There are more eighth notes here, with grace notes almost at random. Let's not feel restricted by rules, so just add grace notes when the mood strikes and where it feels right.

Lick 4

The quarter-note triplets in Lick 4 is an example of another way to expand on your solo.

Photo by Heinrich Klaffs

Keyboardist **Billy Preston** was one of the top session musicians of the 1960s and '70s, having played with artists like Little Richard, Sam Cooke, Ray Charles, The Rolling Stones, Sly & the Family Stone, King Curtis, and The Beatles. Preston was a specialist on the Hammond organ and was the only musician to be credited on a Beatles recording other than the group's four main members.

Photo by Silvio Tanaka

Nicknamed "The Killer," **Jerry Lee Lewis** is one of the pioneers of rock and roll. Lewis recorded his classic hits "Whole Lotta Shakin' Goin' On" and "Great Balls of Fire" at the legendary Sun Studio in Memphis, TN. Lewis was known as a wild showman on the piano and was inducted into the Rock and Roll Hall of Fame in 1986.

Track 2 (Full Mix)
Track 2A (Rhythm Section Only)

Be Good, Johnny

Early Rock and Roll ♩ = 160

Roadmap

1 chorus of head, 2 choruses of piano solo, 2 choruses of guitar solo, 2 choruses of sax solo, 1 chorus of head.

Overview

"Be Good, Johnny" pays homage to one of the greatest rock and roll pianists ever, Johnnie Johnson. Johnnie was inducted into the Rock and Roll Hall of Fame for his work with Chuck Berry. Johnson was one of the fathers of the 1950s rock and roll piano sound. Although he took a back seat to Chuck and wasn't a solo artist like Jerry Lee Lewis or Little Richard, Johnson's performances belong right up there with the best of them.

- Key: C Major
- BPM: 160
- Bars: 37
- Feel: Early blues, rock and roll
- Scale: C Blues

Listening Suggestions

Chuck Berry: "Sweet Little Sixteen"
You can hear Johnnie Johnson jamming in the background of this song—so perfect and so tasty. Listen carefully to some of the stuff he's doing, as it is mixed fairly low and easy to miss. There are so many Chuck Berry tunes to choose from, but this is a good place to start.

Right-Hand Fingering

Part 2

F, C: 5/3, 1, 4/2, 1, 3/2, 4/2
G riff: 5/3, 4/2, 1, 5, 3, 2, 1, 5/2, 2
C riff: 2/5, 5/2, 5/2, 1/4

Part 3

F: 5/3
C triplets: 5/1, 5/2, 5/2, 5/2, 5/3
G: 5/1, 5/1, 5/1

Pocket

Just think "1&–2&–3&–4&–1" over and over again in the beginning of this tune. You don't want to swing or shuffle here, just play straight and think 1950s rock and roll piano the entire time. This one is simple, slick, and old school.

Chords in the Tune

C, F, G

Soloing

This one is performed like Jerry Lee Lewis's "Whole Lotta Shakin' Goin' On," typical of early rock and roll piano parts. You want to think fast, bluesy, old-school Chuck Berry and definitely want to let loose with the triplets and runs. But, you can also play tastefully without necessary pounding as fast as possible. Just mix it up.

Lick 1

This one features old-school, fast triplets in the upper register. You'll be playing quickly here, so try to lock the beginning notes (just after the grace note) with each quarter note in the left hand to make it as tight as possible. You can virtually play the entire series of licks in order as one complete solo.

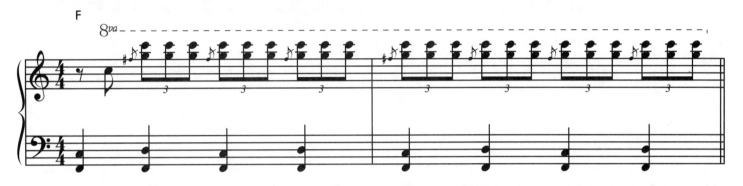

Lick 2

Here are more triplets but with some movement. This one is much trickier than Lick 1.

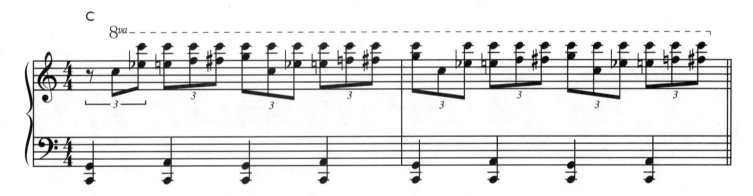

Lick 3

Lick 3 is just a nice little set of 6ths with an old-school turnaround over the V chord to bring the solo back to the I chord.

Track 3 (Full Mix)
Track 3A (Rhythm Section Only)

BABY BLUE

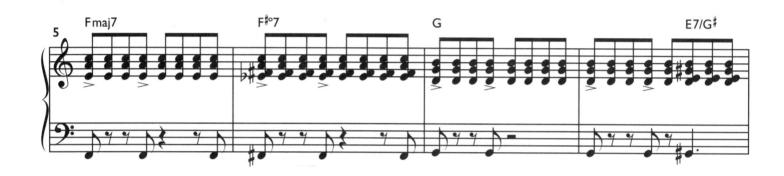

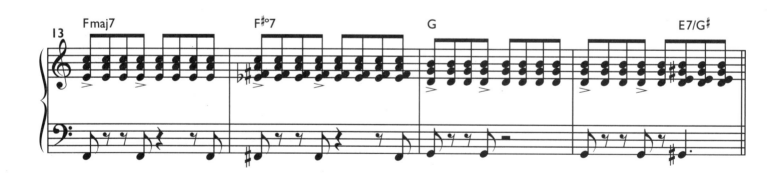

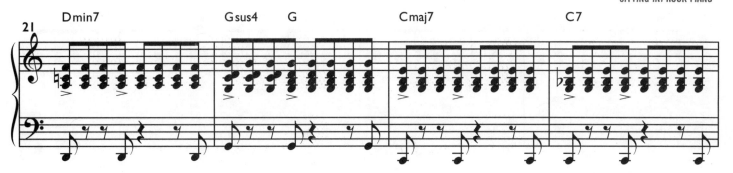

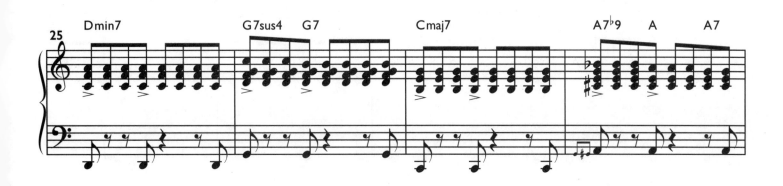

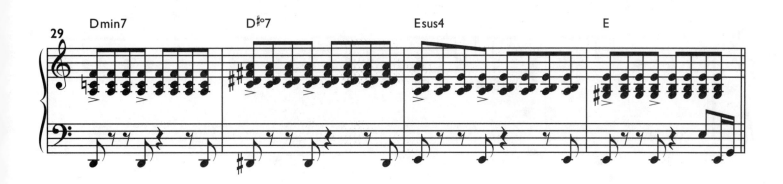

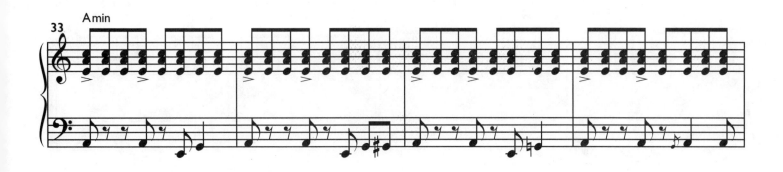

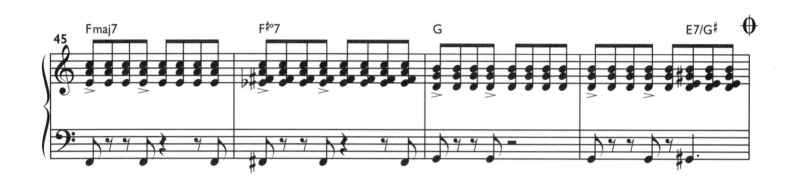

Play 6 times

D.S. al Coda

Roadmap

2 choruses of head, 2 choruses of sax solo, 2 choruses of guitar solo, 2 choruses of keyboard solo, 2 choruses of head, coda.

Overview

The Wurlitzer and Fender Rhodes electric pianos are a big part of rock and roll music. These instruments left a stamp on many iconic songs from the 1960s and '70s, with bands like Pink Floyd, The Beatles, and Led Zeppelin incorporating them into their sound. On "Baby Blue," I added a phaser to the piano to give us a sound that's similar to the keyboards in "The Logical Song" by Supertramp and "Blinded by the Light" by Manfred Mann's Earth Band. The idea behind "Baby Blue" is to put strong accents on beat 1 and the "&" of beat 2: DA, da, da, DA, da, da, da, da (or: **1&–2&–3&–4&**).

- Key: A Minor
- BPM: 109
- Bars: 57
- Feel: Rock
- Scale: A Minor Blues

Listening Suggestions

Supertramp: "The Logical Song"
The keyboard sound on the intro to this song captivated me the first time I heard it. It was a Wurlitzer electric piano with added chorus effect—how simple and perfect. The catchy right-hand part is just a C Minor chord pumping away.

Right-Hand Fingering

Part 1
E, A, C: 1, 3, 5
D♯, F♯, A, C: 1, 2, 3, 5
D, G, B: 1, 2, 4
D, E, G♯, B: 1, 2, 3, 5

Part 2
C, F, A: 1, 3, 5
D, F, G, C: 1, 2, 3, 5
D, F, G, C: 1, 2, 3, 5
B, E, G: 1, 2, 4
C♯, E, G, B♭: 1, 2, 3, 5
C♯, E, A: 1, 2, 4
C♯, E, G: 1, 2, 3
C, F, A: 1, 2, 4
G, C, D, G: 1, 2, 3, 5
G, B, D, G: 1, 2, 3, 5
G, B, E: 1, 2, 4
G, B♭, E: 1, 2, 4

Part 3
C, F, A: 1, 3, 5
D, F, G, C: 1, 2, 3, 5
D, F, G, C: 1, 2, 3, 5
B, E, G: 1, 2, 4
C♯, E, G, B♭: 1, 2, 3, 5
C♯, E, A: 1, 2, 4
C♯, E, G: 1, 2, 3
C, F, A: 1, 2, 4
C, D♯, F♯, A: 1, 2, 3, 5
A, B, E, A: 1, 2, 4, 5
A, B, E: 1, 2, 4
G♯, B, E: 1, 2, 4

Left-Hand Fingering

Part 1

E, G, A: 4, 2, 1
E, G, G♯, A: 4, 3, 2, 1
A, G, F: 1, 2, 3
F, F♯, F♯: 3, 2, 2
F♯, G, G: 2, 1, 1
G, G, G♯: 1, 1, 2

Part 2

D, G, C, A: 4, 1, 5, 1
D, G, C, C: 4, 1, 5, 1

Part 3

D, G, C, A: 4, 1, 5, 1
D, D♯, E, E, G: 4, 3, 3, 4, 2

Pocket

The left hand plays an important role in "Baby Blue," as it's carrying the melody (which is almost always played in the right hand). If you were going to sing the melody, you would likely sing the left-hand part in this song. As mentioned earlier, the key to this pocket is to put strong accents on beat 1 and the "&" of 2. The left hand can be slinky and move between legato and staccato on occasion.

Chords in the Tune

Am, Fmaj7, F♯°7, G, E7/G♯, Dm7, G7sus4, G7, Cmaj7, A7, A, Gsus4, C7, A7♭9, D♯°7, Esus4, E

Soloing

The A Minor Blues and A Minor Pentatonic scales work really well here. Due to the simplicity of those scales by nature (mostly white keys), try experimenting: start soloing on the 2nd tone of the scale, use 4ths, 5ths, etc. "Baby Blue" is a good song to try new things on, which may inspire you to take different approaches to more complex pieces. If you stumble upon something new (theme, rhythm, melody, etc.) that you like, make note of it.

Lick 1

Full, rich chords start off the solo with a hint of a melodic theme.

Lick 2

Here, after a quick eighth-note rest, we come in strong with a cluster of 32nd notes. You'll notice the melodic theme after you play all four bars.

Lick 3

On this one, you will really be flying out of the gate. There's a descending run of 6ths until the last bar, where you finish on an open A5 chord in the right hand that brings us back to the tonic.

Track 4 (Full Mix)
Track 4A (Rhythm Section Only)

JAKE'S THEME

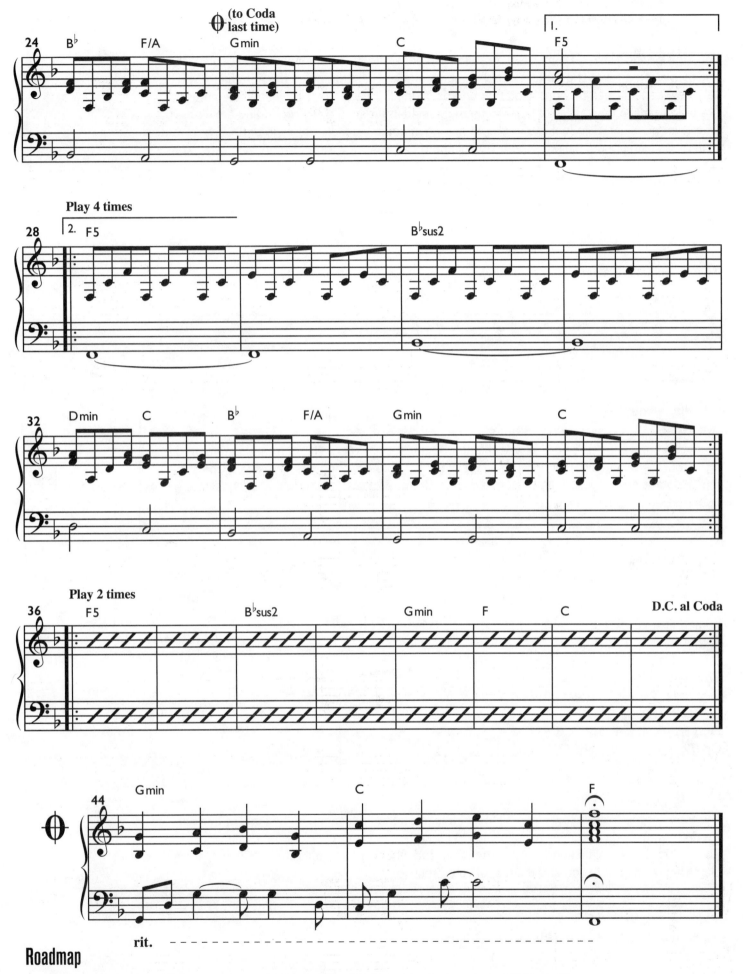

Roadmap

1 chorus of head, 2 choruses of sax solo, 2 choruses of guitar solo, 2 choruses of keyboard solo, 1 chorus of head, coda.

Overview

The idea behind "Jake's Theme" is to grab the listener's attention right away. We accomplish this by playing a repeating pattern of eighth notes at a very fast tempo. In the right hand, you vary between an open 5 chord and other chords. In the left hand, you play just whole notes. I've tried to make the cluster of notes in the right hand interesting by incorporating a melody whenever possible. Billy Joel is a master at playing intricate yet melodic piano parts. If you want to impress with speed, melody, and beautiful chord progressions, listen to Joel.

- Key: F Major
- BPM: 190
- Bars: 46
- Feel: Fast pop/classical
- Scale: F Major scale (see below)

Listening Suggestions

Billy Joel: "Summer, Highland Falls"
A popular song with hard core Billy Joel fans, "Summer, Highland Falls" makes a statement right from the beginning. Not only does Joel show that he's got chops, but his chord changes and melodies are so beautifully intertwined. If you've never heard it before, this song might become your new favorite.

Right-Hand Fingering

Part 1
F5 and B♭sus2: 1, 2, 5, 1, 2, 5, 1, 2, 4, 1, 2, 5, 1, 2, 4, 2
Dm: 5/3, 1, 2, 5/3
C: 5/3, 1, 2, 5/3
B♭: 5/3, 1, 2, 5/3
F/A: 5/3, 1, 2, 3
Gm: 3/2, 1, 4/2, 1, 5/3, 1, 3/2, 1
C: 3/2, 1, 4/2, 1, 5/3, 1.5/3, 1

Part 2
Dm: 4/2, 1, 2, 4, 1, 2, 5
C/E: 1, 2, 3, 5
F: 1, 2, 4, 5
Gm: 3/2, 1, 2, 3, 5/3, 4/2, 3/2, 1
F: 5/3, 1, 2, 3, 5/3, 4/2, 3/2, 1
C: 3/2, 1, 2, 3, 5, 3, 2, 1

Ending
Gm: 3/1, 4/1, 5/1
C: 3/1, 4/1, 5/1
F: 1, 2, 3, 5

Pocket

The term "pocket" refers to the overall feel of a tune's accompaniment. In the case of this tune, we don't want to give you any rules to stick to other than to always think about dynamics. Always play the simplest song with feeling: soft, loud, accents, etc. Just have fun with it, and play what feels right to you and the rest of your group.

Chords in the Tune
F5, B♭sus2, Dm, C, B♭, F/A, Gm, C, A7/C♯, C/E, F

Soloing

The F Major Pentatonic scale works perfectly in "Jake's Theme," but you'll find that the other notes of the F Major scale (B♭, E) work well, too. The 7th tone in the scale (E), which you'll find in the main theme at bar 2, is especially good to use here.

When soloing on "Jake's Theme," it's best to maintain the style and pattern defined in the song. It's a very busy piano piece, so you don't want to lose the feel of the tune during the solo by letting the bottom drop out. Strive to play something melodic, especially on a song like this, which has a strong melodic undertone.

Lick 1

This lick expands on the opening theme, so it's really just another variation of that pattern, highlighted by the addition of a few 32nd notes.

Lick 2

This example shows how you can take a theme and make it sound completely different just by accenting certain notes to create a new pattern.

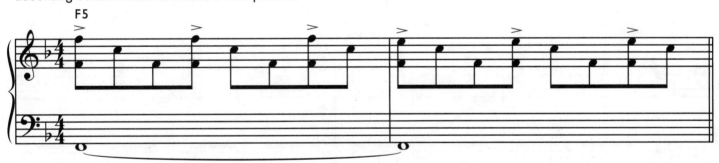

Lick 3

This one mixes up descending and ascending 6ths and is just another approach and motif that you can use.

Track 5 (Full Mix)
Track 5A (Rhythm Section Only)

THE MASTER OF DARKNESS

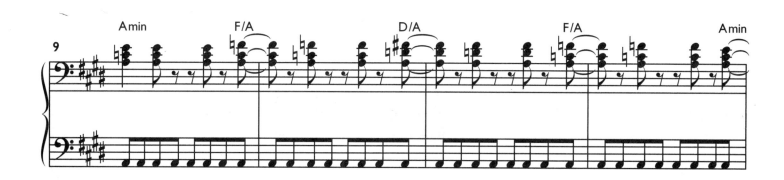

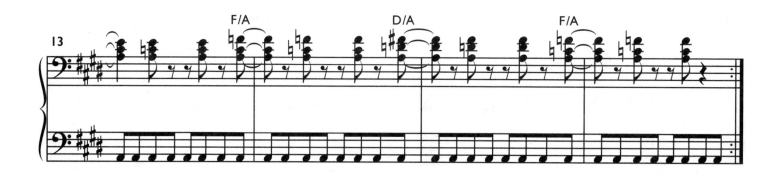

Roadmap

1 chorus of head, 1 chorus of keyboard solo, 1 chorus of guitar solo, 1 chorus of keyboard solo, 1 chorus of guitar solo, 1 chorus of head, coda.

Overview

In "The Master of Darkness," think of yourself as the guitar player, laying down heavy, dirty power chords and shredding as the soloist when the time arrives. This piece is played in the style of Jon Lord, the brilliant keyboardist from Deep Purple. Known for his ferocious Hammond organ playing, Lord incorporated classical and baroque themes into a rock and roll/heavy metal setting. He also got the dirtiest, raunchiest sounds out of his Leslie speaker by running it into a Marshall amplifier. Lord's sound worked really well in conjunction with the electric guitarist in his band, Ritchie Blackmore. Lord could stand side by side and solo in the same manner as Blackmore.

- Key: E
- BPM: 126
- Bars: 33
- Feel: 1970s heavy metal organ
- Scale: E Minor

Listening Suggestions

Deep Purple: "Perfect Strangers"
Listen to that intro. Who wouldn't want that sound from their organ? This is a great reference track for how to play a supporting role in a band. The organ doesn't stand out too much (other than the intro), but it does fill the sound in the best possible way. Jon Lord manages to get in a synth solo at the end though.

Right-Hand Fingering

Part 1

E5: 2, 4
F5/E: 2, 5
D5/E: 1, 3
E5: 2, 4
E5: 1, 2
G/C: 1, 2

Part 2

Am: 1, 2, 3
F/A: 1, 2, 4
D/A: 1, 2, 4

Pocket

Think heavy metal on the keyboards for "The Master of Darkness," with open chords pulsating through to complement the bass, drums, and guitar. Pounding quarter notes in the left hand replicate (and double) the bass guitar, while the right hand starts with power chords, replicating (and doubling) the electric guitar.

Chords in the Tune

E5, F5/E, D5/E, C/E, Am, F/A, D/A

Soloing

Lick 1

This one features straight-ahead 16th notes. Put a slight accent on beats 1 and 2.

Lick 2

Lick 2 is similar to the opening of the song. It's not a traditional single-note solo, but it is another way to expand on the original idea.

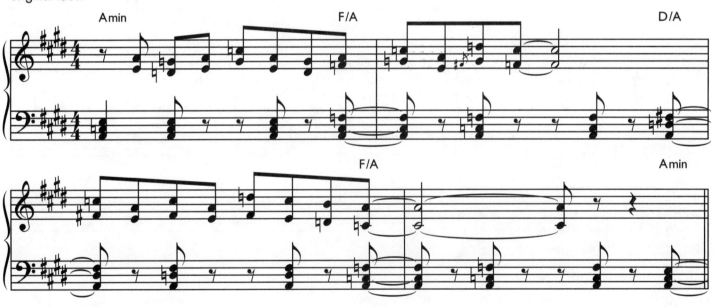

Lick 3

This lick uses very fast ascending trills which are intended to create more of a "wash" of sound. I like this one because it uses a much different approach than a traditional solo, thus opening up more ideas and inspiration.

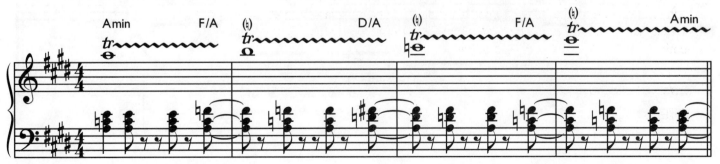

Track 6 (Full Mix)
Track 6A (Rhythm Section Only)

NOW THAT'S A FIRE!

Rock & Roll Blues ♩ = 150

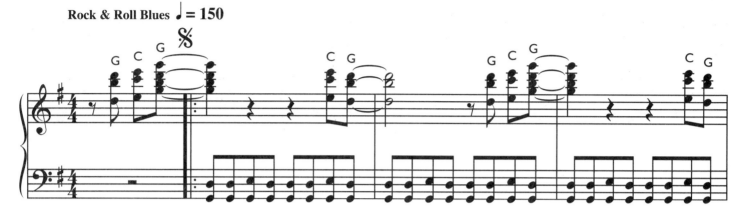

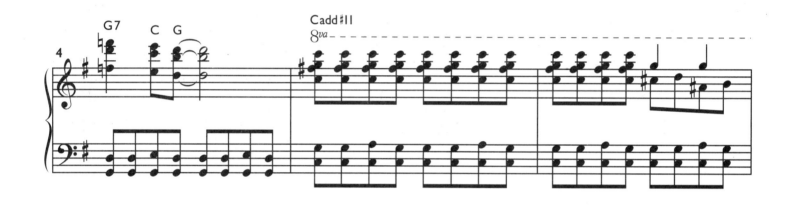

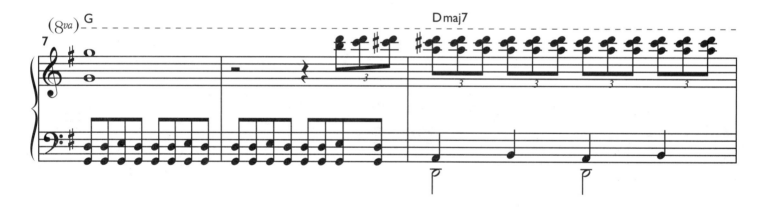

Play 5 Times

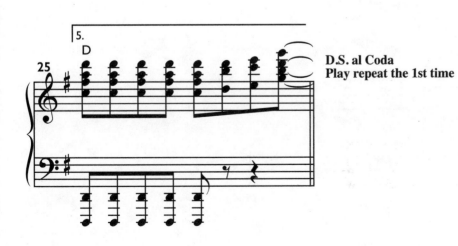

D.S. al Coda
Play repeat the 1st time

Roadmap

2 choruses of head, 1 chorus of keyboard solo, 1 chorus of sax solo, 1 chorus of guitar solo, 1 chorus of sax solo, 1 chorus of guitar solo, 2 choruses of head, coda.

Overview

"Now That's a Fire!" is a throwback to early 1950s rock and roll, when Little Richard and Jerry Lee Lewis were taking the music world by storm. If I had to choose one artist to profile for a rock and roll piano book, it would be Little Richard—not only for his piano playing but also for his singing style and originality. In "Now That's a Fire!," your left hand follows a traditional I–IV–V progression, while the right hand plays a screaming part. This is rock and roll piano in its purest form.

- Key: G Major
- BPM: 150
- Bars: 26
- Feel: 1950s rock and roll
- Scale: G Blues

Listening Suggestions

Little Richard: "Lucille"
Little Richard is one of the most important figures in rock and roll music. So much so, I've included him in this book and my previous book (*Sitting In: Blues Piano*). I can't say enough about him and what a huge influence and originator he was.

Right-Hand Fingering

Part 1

G: 1, 3, 5
C: 1, 4, 5
G: 1, 2, 3, 5

Part 2

C: 1, 2, 3, 5
Riff in bar 7: 5/2, 5/3, 5/2, 5/2

Pocket

You can play it a little loosey-goosey on this one. But, as heavy and fast as the right-hand octaves are played at times, feel that downbeat and try not to let the train get off the track. By keeping the left hand steady on the beat, you have a little more freedom to run wild in the right hand.

Chords in the Tune

G, C, G7, C#11, Dmaj7, D7

Soloing

You can weave in and out of the blues and major pentatonic scales on this tune. Have fun with trying minor 2nds, clusters, and major 6ths. The left hand is very simple with open voicings, so you can add some tension in the right hand. This fits naturally with the musical style of the period.

Lick 1

Lick 1 features a G Blues scale. In the first half, the right hand plays eighth notes up and down the scale with a high G on top throughout. During the second half, you'll find a pair of flat-3rds and flat-5ths before you return to the original theme.

Lick 2

This lick highlights the cluster approach, where you leave some space, come in on the upbeat, etc. There are endless voicings and beats to play off of here.

Lick 3

This one is played near the high register of the piano for that early rock and roll sound. The second part of the lick is an example of what you can play when you move from the V chord to the I chord. Frequently, you would hear fast descending runs (usually octaves) at the end of a solo or introduction in this style.

Track 7 (Full Mix)
Track 7A (Rhythm Section Only)

PARACHUTE

Rock with Heavy Beat, in 2 ♩ = 158

Roadmap

1 chorus of head, 1 chorus of keyboard solo, 1 chorus of sax solo, 1 chorus of guitar solo, 1 chorus of head, coda.

Overview

"Parachute" takes its root from 1970s rock and roll piano, à la early Elton John. Your approach on this piece is to think bluesy and funky, keeping a rock and roll foundation. Elton plays great, straight-ahead rock and roll piano, and when he breaks off into a solo, it is a thing of beauty. He has *the* feel. In this song, the right hand plays a funky and bluesy part over a steady left hand, which is just laying down quarter notes on the beat.

- Key: C
- BPM: 152
- Bars: 16
- Feel: Rock and roll, beat-driven and bluesy
- Scale: C Blues

Listening Suggestions

Elton John: "Take Me to the Pilot"
One of Elton John's earliest recordings, the intro to "Take Me to the Pilot" captures his rock and funky feel right out of the gate. Even though there are strings and guitars in this track, the piano and vocals cut through just perfectly. This is a raw and powerful track.

Right-Hand Fingering

Part 1

C, E, G, C: 1, 2, 3, 5
C, F, A, C: 1, 2, 4, 5
C, E♭, G♭, C: 1, 2, 3, 5
C, E, G, C: 1, 2, 3, 5
D, F, B♭, D: 1, 2, 4, 5
C, F, A, C: 1, 2, 4, 5
C/G: 1, 2, 3, 5
G: 1, 2, 4, 5

Bar 9

C, E♭/C, E, C/C: 1, 2/5, 2, 1

Left-Hand Fingering

Octaves: 5, 1

Pocket

After you listen to Elton John's "Take Me to the Pilot," you'll really get a sense of where "Parachute" is at. It's only the piano in the beginning, and this is where you'll establish the feel of the song. You are creating a beat-driven piece with both hands. The left hand will continue to lay it down before the right hand breaks off a bit (especially when soloing).

Chords in the Tune

C, Dm7, Cdim/E♭, C/E, B♭/F, F, C/G, G

Soloing

When approaching your solo, keep the left hand straight and on the beat, sticking with quarter notes. Use the space in between to experiment with the right hand. Try trills, broken chords, 32nd notes—there are endless possibilities. You can play straight-ahead rock and roll à la Jerry Lee Lewis, bluesy like Ray Charles, or go to New Orleans like Dr. John. Try using the C Blues and C Pentatonic scales.

Lick 1

Lick 1 establishes a somewhat funky feel by starting on the "&" of beat 1 and by using some of the notes of the blues scale.

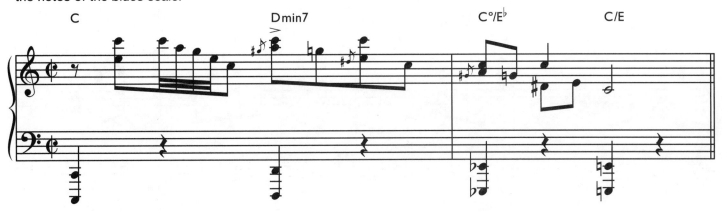

Lick 2

This one starts with the dominant 7th chord (C7) and then finishes with an octave run using notes from the C Blues scale.

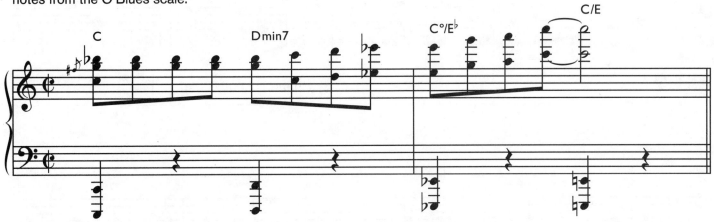

Lick 3

Lick 3 features an always-fun "cluster" chord, as I like to call it. This one is a throwback to Jerry Lee Lewis for a brief moment, and then we're off to a quick pair of 16th notes. When I start with a riff that is somewhat atonal like this, I like to finish with something melodic.

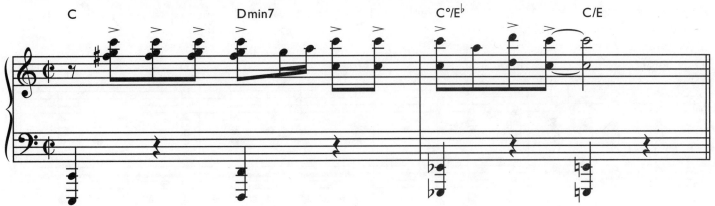

Track 8 (Full Mix)
Track 8A (Rhythm Section Only)

THE JERSEY SHORE

Mid Tempo/Classic Rock Ballad ♩ = 86

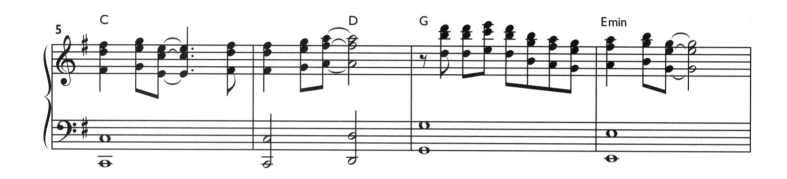

Roadmap

2 choruses of head, 2 choruses of sax solo, 2 choruses of guitar solo, 2 choruses of keyboard solo, 2 choruses of head, coda.

Overview

"The Jersey Shore" is an example of a dramatic, yet simple, four-chord progression that aims to create an arena rock-type of energy. Bruce Springsteen is a master of that type of energy, and this song borrows from that. The intro is all yours, and then you build with the band during the B section. Think big and dramatic, with full right-hand octaves ringing over the band and through the crowd (with lighters and cell phones in the air).

- Key: G Major
- BPM: 86
- Bars: 29

- Feel: Slow, classic rock power ballad
- Scale: G Major

Listening Suggestions

Bruce Springsteen: "Backstreets"
Keyboardist Roy Bittan, nicknamed "The Professor," is one of the best at creating long, beautiful, melodic intros. A longtime member of Bruce Springsteen's E Street Band, "Backstreets" was one of the first songs Bittan recorded with "The Boss." Bittan's parts have become an essential part of the E Street Band sound.

Right-Hand Fingering

Part 1

D, B, D: 1, 3, 5
E, C, E: 1, 4, 5
B, G, B: 1, 4, 5
A, F♯, A: 1, 3, 5
G, E, G: 1, 3, 5

Part 2 (Finger Variation)

F♯, D, F♯: 1, 3, 5
G, E, G: 1, 4, 5
E, C, E: 1, 3, 5
G, E, G: 1, 4, 5
A, F♯, A: 1, 4, 5

Part 3

G, B, G: 1, 2, 5
G, C, G: 1, 2, 5
G, D, G: 1, 2, 5
G, E, G: 1, 4, 5

Part 4

G, B, G: 1, 2, 5
F♯, B, D, F♯: 1, 2, 3, 5
G, C, E: 1, 2, 4
D, G, A, D: 1, 2, 3, 5
D, F♯, A, D: 1, 2, 3, 5

Pocket

"The Jersey Shore" features full octaves. The band takes a back seat here, so don't hesitate or hold back. A nice, simple melody should be played straight and on the beat. When you hit the B section, you are in a much lower register, playing together with the band—loud, legato chord changes.

Chords in the Tune

G, Em, C, D, Am7, G/B, Bm, Dsus4, D, Csus2, G5/D

Soloing

Soloing on "The Jersey Shore" is a great opportunity to play something melodic, which is something I like to strive for when given the opportunity. The chord changes before transitioning to the IV and V chords are fairly open (going back and forth between G and Em). Keep it slow, feel the space, and don't feel like you have to play on top of every beat. There is *a lot* of room here.

Lick 1

This is an example of how you can start your solo: emphasize the main intro melody by entering after the first eighth-note rest. Also, try incorporating octaves so you're not distancing yourself too far away from the theme out of the gate.

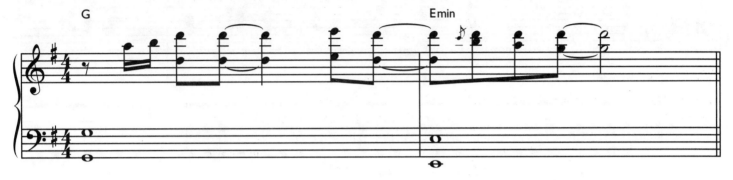

Lick 2

Here's an example of how to use a chord (C/G) that's not in the song. It works here within a solo context because you're always free to break out a bit, and incorporating a chord that's not in the song does just that. Grace notes can be tasty here and will add some shine when used properly (after beat 3 in this example).

Lick 3

Here are some 16th-note runs you can build up to. Again, try to keep a melodic sense in your playing (especially on ballads), even when using extra notes within a given phrase.

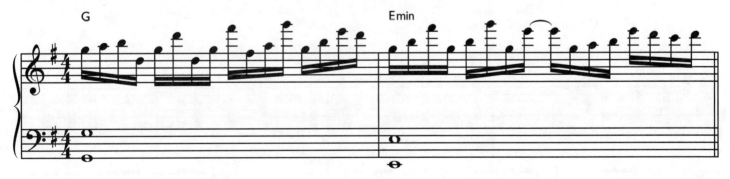

Track 9 (Full Mix)
Track 9A (Rhythm Section Only)

Friday Night

80's Pop Rock ♩ = 116

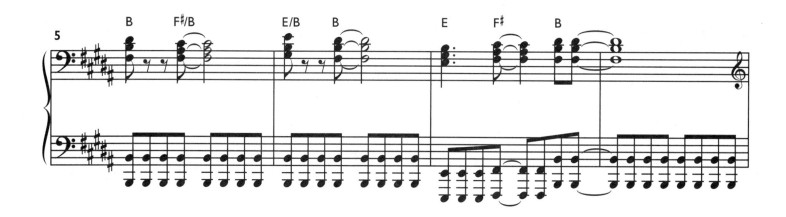

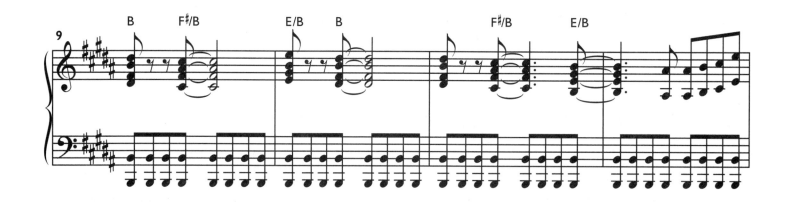

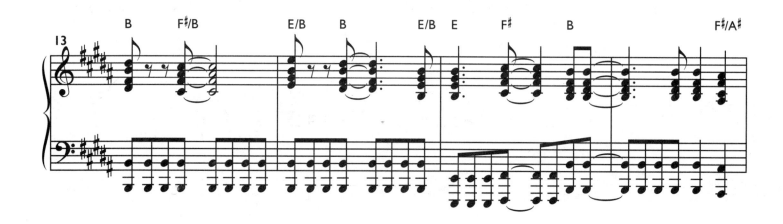

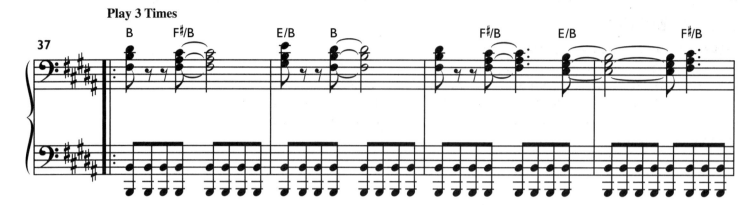

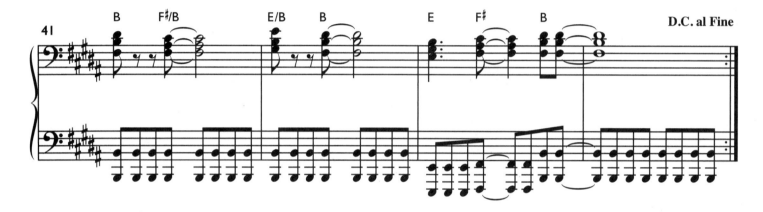

Roadmap

1 chorus of head, 1 chorus of guitar solo, 1 chorus of sax solo, 1 chorus of keyboard solo, 1 chorus of head.

Overview

With "Friday Night," you get to be the keyboardist in that early 1980s hair band you've always dreamed about. There are several bands and artists that played in this style, including Survivor, Journey, and Phil Collins. Some of the songs from this era are forgettable, but the great thing about this period is that almost every band had a keyboard player. Synthesizers dominated pop radio, and parts like the ones in "Friday Night" were everywhere. Here, you'll be playing repetitive quarter or eighth notes that pump along with the bass player, and ever-changing triads in the right hand with the guitar player.

- Key: B
- BPM: 116
- Bars: 44
- Feel: 1980s pop/rock, synth
- Scale: B Major

Right-Hand Fingering

Part 1

B: 1, 2, 4
F#/B: 1, 2, 3
E/B: 1, 2, 5
E/B: 1, 2, 3
E: 1, 2, 3
F#: 1, 2, 3

Part 2

B: 1, 2, 4, 5
F#/B: 1, 2, 3, 5
E/B: 1, 2, 3, 5

E: 1, 2, 3, 5
F#: 1, 2, 4, 5
B: 1, 2, 3, 5

Part 3

G#m: 1, 2, 3, 5
F#/A#: 1, 2, 4, 5
F#/A#: 1, 2, 4, 5
E/B: 1, 2, 3, 5
B: 1, 2, 4, 5
C#m: 1, 2, 4, 5
B/D#: 1, 2, 4, 5
D#, C# (single notes): 5, 4

B/F#: 1, 2, 3
F#: 1, 2, 3

Ending Lick

E: 5, 4, 2
F#: 5, 4, 2, 1
B: 1, 2, 3, 5
B: 5/2, 3, 1, 3, 2
E: 5, 3, 2
F#: 1, 2, 3, 5
B: 1, 2, 3

Left-Hand Fingering

Octaves: 1, 5

Pocket

In a nutshell, you are playing like both the bass and guitar player on "Friday Night." The left hand plays straight eighth notes without any variation (like a bass player), while the right hand plays chords (à la a guitar player). Make sure you get those rests in there, and don't hold out the chords—they are eighth notes not dotted quarters. This is what gives the song impact and creates that '80s pop/rock sound.

Chords in the Tune

B/F#, F#/B, E/B, B, E, F#, G#m, F#/A, C#m, B/D#

Soloing

Although there's no strong melody in the pumping, main part of the song, there's a foundation there that lends itself to supporting a melodic line. You can almost sing themes to yourself while playing.

Lick 1

Here's an example of bringing in a melody and filling it up in a solo with 16th notes.

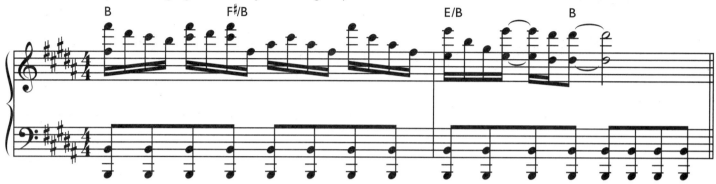

Lick 2

In this example, I play the usual right-hand pattern in the left hand, while embellishing in the right hand.

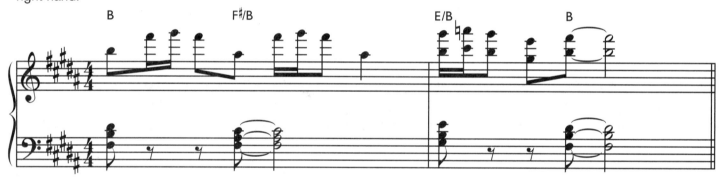

Lick 3

Keeping with the left-hand pattern from Lick 2, the right hand plays one note at a time (although quite fast) here. This kind of solo would work well on a synthesizer.

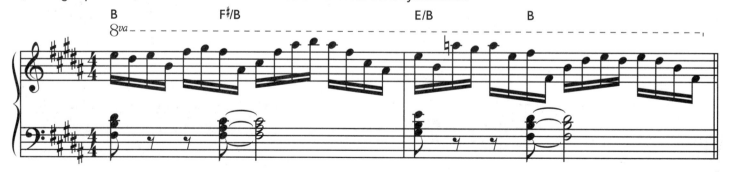

Roadmap

1 chorus of head, 1 chorus of guitar solo, 1 chorus of sax solo, 1 chorus of keyboard solo,
1 chorus of head, coda.

Overview

"Round and Round (Here We Go)" was influenced by a great contemporary artist, Ben Folds.
For many, he kind of filled the void of a modern day Elton John on the radio airwaves. Not
only can Folds play great rock and roll piano, but he can write a beautiful love song as well.
His approach is very raw, and he puts it all out there. I've heard he's pretty hard on his pianos
during concerts—Jerry Lee Lewis would be proud! This song captures Folds' uptempo, rock
and roll style. The piano drives this one all the way through.

- Key: A
- BPM: 114
- Bars: 40
- Feel: Rock and roll
- Scale: A Blues

Listening Suggestions

Ben Folds Five: "One Angry Dwarf and 200 Solemn Faces"
Ben Folds brings back great rock and roll piano on this song. "One Angry Dwarf and 200 Solemn Faces" features a super tasty intro with wonderful interplay between the right and left hands. Also, check out the piano solo—you can tell Folds is just having a blast. This piece was so fresh and inspiring when I first heard it.

Right-Hand Fingering

Part 1

A: 5/1, 2, 1, 1
G/A: 1, 2, 5
D/A: 1, 2, 4

Part 2

G/A: 1, 2, 5
D/A: 1, 2, 4
A: 1, 3, 1

Part 3

A: 1, 2, 3, 5
C7: 1, 2, 4, 5
D7: 1, 2, 4, 5
F: 1, 2, 4
G: 1, 2, 5
A: 1, 2, 3, 5

Part 4

A, G/A (16th-note runs): 5, 3, 1
F/A (16th-note runs): 5, 2, 1

Left-Hand Fingering

Part 1

Octaves throughout: 5, 1

Pocket

The left hand does not vary in time or rhythm; you just want to keep a solid foundation here. The right hand (on the other hand, get it?) is busy at times but always maintains a good feel for the beat. Keep it bluesy, play with dynamics, and incorporate strong accents—all while locking in with that steady left hand.

Chords in the Tune

A, G/A, D/A, E/A, E, G, D, A5, Dm(maj7), B°/F, E7, Dsus2/E, Asus4

Soloing

Here are three licks you can try. The first two follow the straight eighth note A–A progression, and Lick 3 follows the chord changes in the B section. I like the blues vibe here, with strong accents now and again for impact. When expanding this on your own, try to come in at different times to start your solo, not just on bar 1, beat 1. Eighth, 16th, and 32nd notes are all here, just to showcase the endless possibilities. Have fun, experiment, and mix things up as much as possible.

Lick 1

This is something Elton John might bang out when he's playing a solo, with back and forth
octaves of eighth notes and a bluesy cluster of runs and broken chords.

Lick 2

Lick 2 is just classic rock and roll. You can intersperse this lick as it suits you, mixing it up with
triplets for a quicker approach.

Lick 3

This lick follows the chord changes in the B section, which is a lot of fun to play. When you are
following chord changes, you definitely have to be aware of the chords you are working with,
but it's okay to branch out a bit and not play the exact notes of the chord as in this example.

Track 11 (Full Mix)
Track 11A (Rhythm Section Only)

LA 2025

Classic Rock, Mid Tempo Ballad ♩ = 132

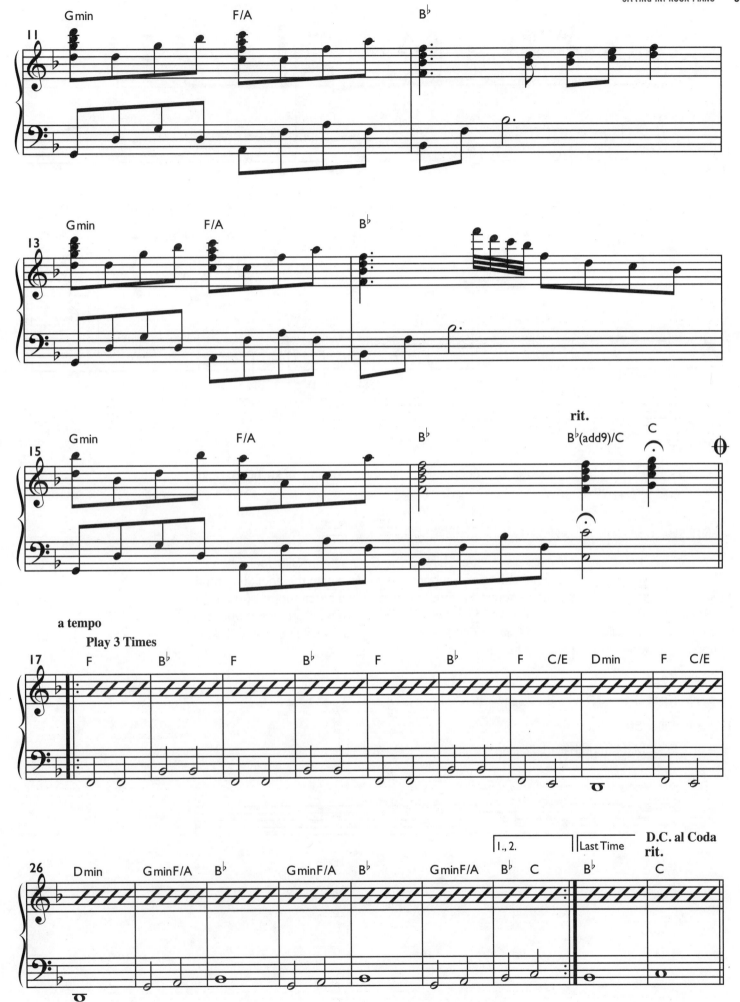

Roadmap

1 chorus of head, 1 chorus of sax solo, 1 chorus of guitar solo, 1 chorus of keyboard solo,
1 chorus of head, coda.

Overview

This piece is a standard rock/pop piano intro. Think Bruce Springsteen, Billy Joel, Elton John, and singer-songwriters who feature and support themselves with the acoustic grand piano. This type of piece can be performed without a band, or any other support (other than a vocalist). The combination of the left and right hand parts create a full and somewhat busy sound, so it will call for some simplicity from the bass and guitars. You'll find they will likely support you with whole notes and textures.

- Key: F
- BPM: 132
- Bars: 39
- Feel: Mid-tempo ballad, flowing
- Scale: F Major

Right-Hand Fingering

Part 1

F: 5/3, 4, 2, 5/3, 4, 5, 4, 3, 2, 1
B♭: 1, 2, 3, 5
B♭sus4: 1, 2, 3, 5
B♭ (descending chords): 1, 3, 5

Part 2

F: 1, 2, 4, 5
C/E: 1, 2, 4, 5
Dm: 1, 2, 4, 5

Part 3

Gm: 1, 2, 3, 5
F/A: 1, 2, 4, 5
B♭: 1, 2, 4, 5
B♭ (ascending 3rds): 2, 3/2, 4/3, 5
B♭ (descending run): 5, 4, 3, 2, 4, 3, 2

Part 4

Gm: 5/2, 1, 3, 5
F/A: 5/2, 1, 2, 5
B♭: 1, 2, 3, 5
C: 1, 2, 3, 5

Ending

B♭: 1, 2, 3, 5
B♭+9: 1, 2, 4, 5
C: 1, 2, 4
F: 1, 2, 3, 5

Left-Hand Fingering

Part 1

F: 5, 2, 1, 2, 1, 2
B♭: 5, 2, 1, 1, 2

Part 2

F, C/E, Dm: 5, 2, 1

Part 3

Gm, F/A, B♭: 5, 2, 1

Pocket

Think singer-songwriter here, in the sense that you are creating the entire musical spectrum by yourself. Don't worry about thinning your chord voicings for fear of clashing with the bass player—they will find a part around you.

Chords in the Tune

F, B♭, B♭sus4, C/E, Dm, Gm, F/A, B♭+9/C, C

Soloing

"LA 2025" has a somewhat busy piano part within itself, and you'll often find yourself supporting a saxophone or guitar solo over this type of piece. There are, however, times when you have an opportunity to embellish and expand on an initial theme, which is the idea here. So when soloing, try to keep the left-hand pattern the same all the way through, and take the right hand and expand on it by bringing in a different melody or breaking up the pattern a bit.

Lick 1

Here you'll be matching the flow of the left hand and changing up the melody a bit.

Lick 2

Instead of single eighth notes, this time you'll be playing fuller, richer chords all the way through.

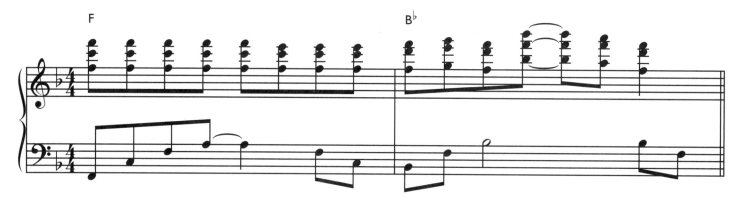

Lick 3

Lick 3 features similar themes from earlier in the piece but starting with a different chord inversion.

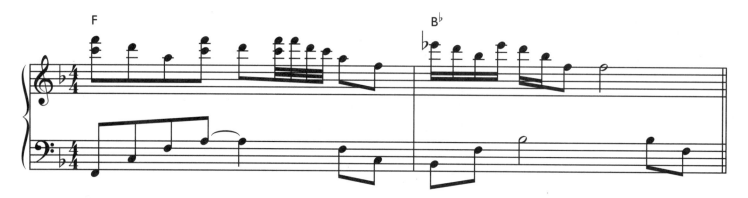

Track 12 (Full Mix)
Track 12A (Rhythm Section Only)

SHOWTIME

Roadmap

1 chorus of head with organ solo, 1 guitar solo, 1 chorus of head with no organ solo, coda.

Overview

"Showtime" is in the style of Emerson, Lake & Palmer, one of the biggest progressive rock bands from the 1970s. This tune is ideally played on the Hammond organ—or a keyboard synthesizer with that sound. The style of "Showtime" leans towards classical symphonic rock. Keith Emerson's keyboard performances were so powerful and theatrical. So in keeping with that theme, feel free to show off your chops and be a little over the top here. I mean, Keith had a flying piano, so the sky's the limit.

- Key: E♭, F
- BPM: 124
- Bars: 58
- Feel: Progressive, organ rock
- Scale: G Minor Pentatonic

Listening Suggestions

Emerson, Lake & Palmer: "Karn Evil 9: 1st Impression, Part 2"
This is one of Emerson, Lake & Palmer's biggest hits, with an organ solo, synth solo, and layers, layers, and more layers. Listen to how the organ follows the vocal melody in the second half of the verse without getting in the singer's way. Keith Emerson's organ part actually enhances the melody and creates a strong, defined keyboard riff—it's always nice if you can create a "part" as opposed to just playing chords. Also, the synth underneath the organ solo is smokin'. There's something for every keyboardist in this song.

Right-Hand Fingering

Part 1

E♭: 1, 2, 4
A♭/E♭: 1, 2, 5
B♭/E♭: 1, 3, 5
F: 1, 2, 4
B♭/F: 1, 2, 5
C/F: 1, 2, 5
B♭/F: 1, 2, 4
B♭5, G♭5: 1, 3, 5
D♭5, E♭5, F5: 1, 2, 5

Part 2

Gm: 1, 2, 3
C/G: 1, 2, 4
G7: 1, 3, 5
Am: 1, 2, 3
D/A: 1, 2, 4
A7: 1, 3, 5

Part 3

Am: 1, 2, 4, 5
A♭+: 1, 2, 3, 5
C/G, C♭5/F♯: 1, 2, 3, 5
C♭, B♭: 1, 2, 3, 5

Part 4

Bars 41–42: 1, 3, 5

Left-Hand Fingering

Part 1

Octaves throughout: 5, 1

Part 2

G, G, C, C, D, F: 5, 1, 3, 3, 2, 1
A, A, D, D, E, F: 5, 1, 3, 3, 2, 1

Part 3

A, E, A, A♭: 5, 2, 1, 1
G, G♭, G♭, G, A♭: 1, 2, 2, 1, 2

Part 4

B♭, A♭, F, D♭, C, D♭: 1, 2, 3, 3, 4, 3
E♭, D♭, B♭: 2, 3, 5

Pocket

For such a big, powerful-sounding track, you really want to focus on playing on the beat with even dynamics for "Showtime." There's not really a moment where things come down dynamically in the tune, other than what you might naturally do when someone is soloing (e.g., the guitar solo in this song). You should play loud—with force—and as strong as the other instruments.

Chords in the Tune

E♭, A♭/E♭, B♭/E♭
F, B♭/F, C/F
B♭5, G♭5, D♭5, E♭5, F5
Gm, C/G, G7
Am, D/A, A7
A♭+, C♭5/F♯
C5, B♭, A♭5

Soloing

In these examples, we are going to focus solely on the right hand. There are four licks, building from the ground up. They are geared towards an organ sound, but a synthesizer would work just as well—especially on Lick 1. As you progress through these, you can really show off some speed as you work you way up to the sextuplets.

Lick 1

Although an organ piece, I actually had a synth in mind for this solo. While a sustaining half note starts things off, pace yourself for more to come.

Lick 2

Here, 16th-note runs follow the chord changes and move through different inversions. Pay attention to the accents.

Lick 3

Like Lick 2, Lick 3 features 16th notes that follow a chord progression. Although similar in appearance to Lick 2, the chord progression in Lick 3 is different and there are no specific accents as the runs are played somewhat evenly.

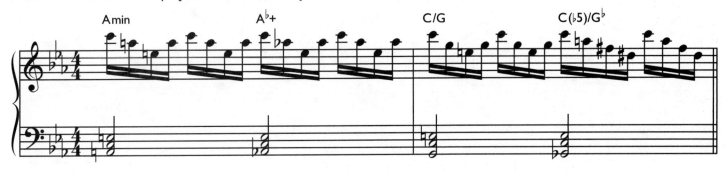

Lick 4

This lick is fast and furious with sextuplets. Pay attention to the accents on the top notes (finger 5) to help stay in time.

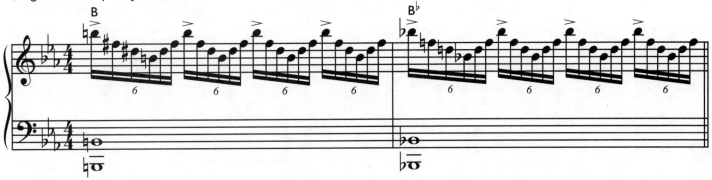

Track 13 (Full Mix)
Track 13A (Rhythm Section Only)

LOVE SONG

Roadmap

1 chorus of head, 1 chorus of keyboard solo, 1 chorus of guitar solo, 1 chorus of keyboard solo, 1 chorus of guitar solo, 1 chorus of head, coda.

Overview

"Love Song" shows how rock and classical themes can blend beautifully together. Many bands over the years have done this, including Emerson, Lake & Palmer, Electric Light Orchestra, and Yes. This song leans more on the rock and roll side, but the string motif in the right hand recalls a classical theme. "Love Song" is to be played with a band, relying heavily on the drums to create that rock and roll foundation.

- •   Key: A Minor
- •   BPM: 150
- •   Bars: 50
- •   Feel: Classical strings, symphonic rock
- •   Scale: A Melodic Minor

Listening Suggestions

Led Zeppelin: "All My Love"
This song contains a beautiful synth solo by Led Zeppelin bassist John Paul Jones. It's a perfect example of mixing things up—not always landing on the tonic or playing eighth, quarter, and dotted quarter notes—and keeping things melodic. When I'm about to park my car and this song comes on the radio, I always have to listen to the solo before shutting off the engine.

Right-Hand Fingering

Part 1

Same fingering for each bar in opening theme: 5, 1, 2, 3, 4, 5, 4, 3

Part 2

Am: 1, 3, 3, 3, 2, 3, 4
E/G♯: 5, 2, 3, 4, 5, 4, 3, 2
Am/G: 4, 3, 2, 1, 4, 3, 2, 1
D, E: 2, 3, 4, 2, 3, 4, 5, 3

Part 3

F: 1, 2, 4, 5
C: 1, 2, 4, 5
Bdim7: 1, 2, 4, 5
E7: 1, 2, 3, 5
C/G: 1, 2, 4, 5
G: 1, 2, 3, 5

Left-Hand Fingering

Part 1

Same fingering for each bar in opening theme: 5, 2, 1, 2, 1, 1, 2, 5

Part 2

Am: 5, 2, 1, 2
E/G♯: 5, 2, 1, 2
Am/G: 5, 2, 1, 2
D: 5, 2, 1
E: 5, 2, 1

Part 3

Octaves: 5, 1

Pocket

Since the band is creating a heavy background rhythm in "Love Song," you should think like J. S. Bach and Rick Wakeman. Easy, right? Both right- and left-hand parts are busy, playing counter melodies (similar to some of the Bach inventions I studied as a child). The B section is pure Led Zeppelin-type rock and roll, with thick and heavy chords playing in unison. You start light, and then dig deep. Another thing to look out for: during the solo section, you'll be playing the string part with your left hand and the synth solo with your right. This is something to take advantage of when you have a two-keyboard setup (or a split preset that you can program if you only have one synth).

Chords in the Tune

Am, G, F, E/G♯, Am/G, D, E, C, Bmin7♭5, E7, C/G

Soloing

There are strong classical overtones in this piece, so you can approach the solos as a string player (using a synth) or as a classical pianist (using a piano or a harpsichord, if you can get your hands on one). Lick 3 is definitely geared towards using the latter style.

Lick 1

Lick 1 breaks things up a bit with a quarter-note rest on the first bar, but it stays within the classical theme by adding a trill. There's nothing too fancy here on the first pass.

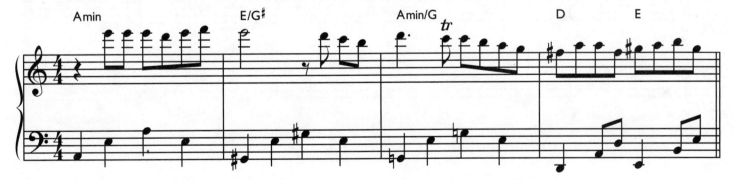

Lick 2

Lick 2 features eighth-note runs that follow the chord progression. It moves at a fast pace, but keep it steady.

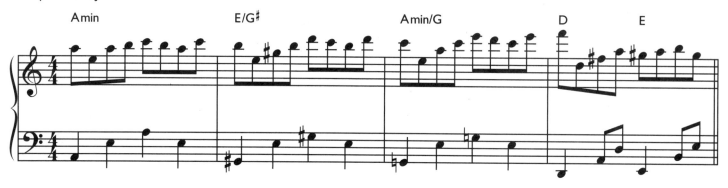

Lick 3

Lick 3 includes strong accents for more variation.

Lick 4

Lick 4 starts on the note B, the 2nd tone of the scale, showing how you don't always have to start on the tonic. This creates some nice tension and is something different to help keep the listener's attention.

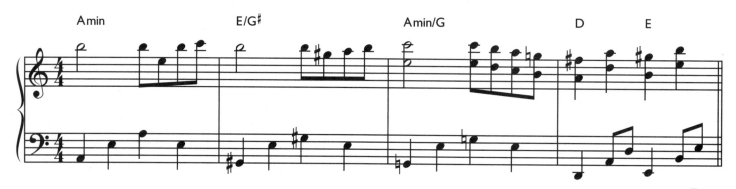

Track 14 (Full Mix)
Track 14A (Rhythm Section Only)

FALLING FORWARD

Prog Rock ♩ = 180

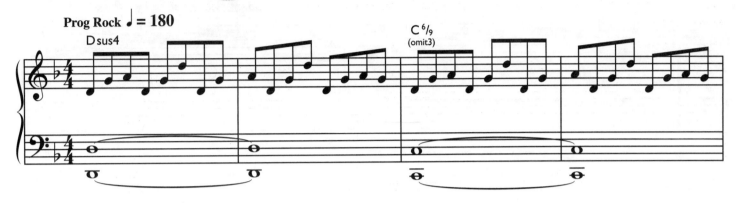

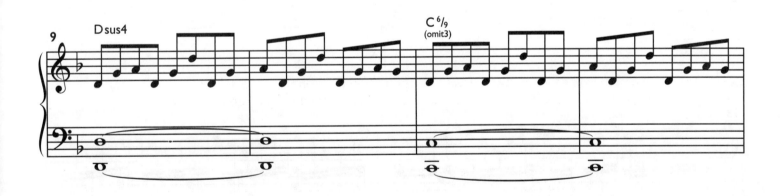

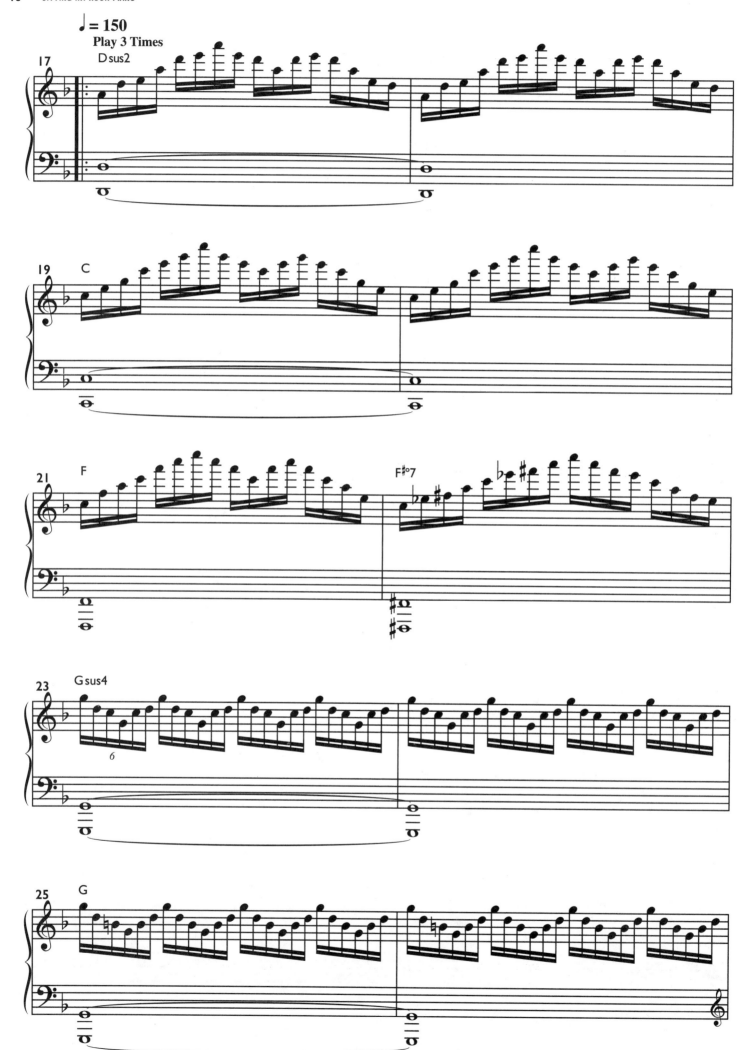

Roadmap

1 chorus of head, 1 chorus of keyboard solo, 1 chorus of guitar solo, 1 chorus of keyboard solo.

Overview

"Falling Forward" takes its inspiration from keyboard virtuoso Rick Wakeman. Most famous for being in the band Yes, Wakeman played a variety of styles. (If you search "Rick Wakeman Solo" on YouTube, you'll see what I mean.) He could fly with the best of them. He could play fast or in an ambient, new age style. Wakeman played piano, electric piano, organ, and synthesizer. You name it, and he covered it—all in dramatic fashion.

- Key: D Minor
- BPM: 180
- Bars: 37
- Feel: Progressive rock
- Scale: D Minor

Listening Suggestions

Rick Wakeman and the New English Rock Ensemble: "Catherine Parr"
This song is nine minutes and 46 seconds of mayhem, in the best possible way. Wakeman has probably influenced every prog-rock keyboard player out there. After listening to this piece, you'll understand why he is always on the list of the most influential keyboard players.

Right-Hand Fingering

Part 1

Dsus4: 1, 2, 3, 1, 2, 5

Part 2

Dm: 1, 2, 3, 1, 2, 3, 5
C: 1, 2, 3, 1, 2, 3, 5
F: 1, 2, 3, 1, 2, 3, 5
F#dim7: 1, 2, 3, 4, 1, 2, 3, 4, 5
G: 5, 3, 2, 1

Part 3

Dm, C: 5, 2, 1
C#dim7: 5, 2, 1 5, 2, 1, 4, 2, 1

Ending (bars 36 and 37)

C#dim7: 5/1, 4, 3, 2, 1, 4
C#dim7: 5/1, 4, 3, 2, 1, 4, 2
Dm: 1, 2, 3, 5

Left-Hand Fingering

Parts 1 and 2

Octaves: 5/1

Part 3

Dm: 5, 2, 1, 2, 3, 4
C: 5, 2, 1, 2, 3, 4
B♭: 5, 2, 1, 1, 2, 1

Ending (bars 35–37)

B♭: 5, 3, 2, 1, 3, 2, 1, 2, 3, 2, 3, 1, 2, 3
C♯dim: 5, 3, 2, 1, 2, 1, 5, 3, 2, 1, 2, 1
Dm: 5/2, 5/1

Pocket

This one starts with a dramatic intro, as the left hand plays whole notes and the right hand plays suspended broken chords. There is a tempo change at bar 17 as you enter (and stay in) solo mode until the end of the solo section.

Chords in the Tune

Dsus4, C5(add6/9), Gsus2, Dm, C, F, F♯dim7, Gsus4, G, B♭, C♯dim7

Soloing

It's not often that you can use the harmonic minor scale, but you'll find moments (Lick 3) where it works here. Otherwise, the D Minor scale works perfectly well. With the following series of licks, we'll be using a few from the actual piece.

Lick 1

This run outlines the Dsus2 chord and is basically a straight arpeggio.

Lick 2

We'll be playing 16th-note sextuplets here. That's right...steady as she goes. Place a slight accent on the top G note of each grouping, which will help you lock into the beat and keep good time.

Lick 3

Here you have a classical-style theme with a tricky little sample of contrary motion at the finish.

Photo by Heinrich Klaffs

With more than 300 million record sales to his credit, Sir **Elton John** is one of the best-selling recording artists of all time. John was a standout among the many notable singer-songwriters that came to prominence in the 1970s. A masterful songwriter as well as pianist, John was inducted into the Rock and Roll Hall of Fame in 1994.

Photo by Aurelio Moraes

Virtuoso keyboardist **Rick Wakeman** is best known for playing in the progressive rock band Yes. Throughout a five-decade-long career—which includes over 90 solo releases—Wakeman has spent time playing with a diverse roster of rock legends, including Lou Reed, Elton John, Cat Stevens, T. Rex, Black Sabbath, and David Bowie.

Track 15 (Full Mix)
Track 15A (Rhythm Section Only)

BREAK IT DOWN

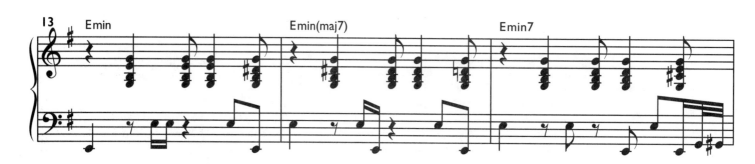

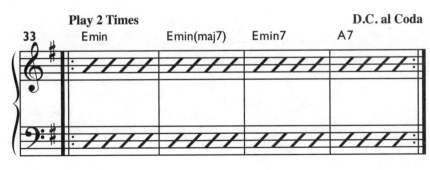

Roadmap

2 choruses of head, 1 chorus of keyboard solo, 1 chorus of sax solo, 1 chorus of guitar solo, 2 choruses of keyboard solo over bars 33–36, 2 choruses of head, coda.

Overview

"Break It Down" opens with a four-bar intro that instantly establishes a blues/funk feel with just three chords. Billy Preston is your inspiration here. Play this with a Clavinet sound and some wah-wah. The sound will inspire your performance, so make sure you dial something in that you like. If you only have one sound to choose from, start with the Clavinet.

- Key: G Major
- BPM: 102
- Bars: 37
- Feel: Rock, funk
- Scale: G Blues

Listening Suggestions

The Rolling Stones, "Doo Doo Doo Doo Doo (Heartbreaker)"
The late, great Billy Preston is just doing his thing here. I don't know if the part or the sound came first, but my guess is that it was this *killer* keyboard sound that inspired the intro part. What gives this song its funky edge is a Clavinet mixed in with an RMI Electra-piano (which creates a harpsichord-type sound). The blend of these two keyboards really created something cool. Oh yeah, and there's a wah-wah on the Clavinet for an added taste of funk.

Right-Hand Fingering

Part 1

G, D, F: 1, 3, 5
F, A♭, B♭, D, F: 1, 2, 3, 4, 5
C, B♭, E, G: 1, 2, 4, 5
G, D, F: 1, 3, 5

Part 2

G, B, E, G: 1, 2, 3, 4, 5
G, B, D♯, G: 1, 2, 4, 5
G, B, D, E: 1, 2, 4, 5
G, C♯, E, G: 1, 2, 4, 5
G, A, C♯, E: 1, 2, 3, 5

Left-Hand Fingering

Octaves: 5, 1

Pocket

The keyboard part in "Break It Down" really leans on the funk side, while the band maintains a rock and roll backdrop. The combination of the sound of the Clavinet and the chord progressions will naturally inspire a funky approach. This is a great thing. Just don't get funky to the point where it changes the feel of the song. Remember, it's still a rock song and you don't need to stand out too much. The coolness factor of your keyboard sound will do plenty.

Chords in the Tune

G7, B♭7, C7, F, G, Em, EmMaj7, Em7, A7/E, A7, G5, C

Soloing

This time around, we've included soloing examples over both sections of the piece. Lick 1 uses the second part of the song, while Licks 2 and 3 use the first part. You will see that there's more of a comp part in the left hand, which follows the chord progressions of the song. Think blues, rock, and a little funk.

Lick 1

We'll take a melodic approach here, along with something different to counterbalance the syncopation in the track.

Lick 2

Here, we emphasize the dominant 7th chord, ending with a simple melody.

Lick 3

This lick takes a slightly gospel approach. You may notice there's a minor 3rd in the opening even though there's no 3rd in the tune. It's used here to show how you can take a dominant 7th and turn it into a minor 7th to create a bluesy and gospel sound.

Comping Riff

The music notation doesn't always match what is played on the recording since I try to vary my comping patterns to keep things interesting. This example shows one of the variations on the recording.

Comping Riff

On the C7 chord, try adding some 16th notes in the right and left hands.